SECRET
OF THE
SINGING
MICE
... AND MORE!

BY ANA MARÍA RODRÍGUEZ

Enslow Publishers, Inc.
40 Industrial Road
Box 398
Berkeley Heights, NJ 07922
USA
http://www.enslow.com

Acknowledgments

The author would like to express her immense gratitude to all the scientists who have contributed to the *Animal Secrets Revealed!* series. Their comments and photos have been invaluable to the creation of these books.

Library of Congress Cataloging-in-Publication Data

Rodriguez, Ana Maria, 1958-
    Secret of the singing mice— and more! / Ana María Rodríguez.
        p. cm. — (Animal secrets revealed!)
    Summary: "Explains how mice use ultrasonic vocalizations to attract mates and details other strange abilities of different types of animals"—Provided by publisher.
    Includes bibliographical references and index.
    ISBN-13: 978-0-7660-2956-9
    ISBN-10: 0-7660-2956-5
    1. Mammals—Juvenile literature. 2. Mammals—Research—Juvenile literature. I. Title.
    QL706.2.R636 2009
    599—dc22   2007039495

Printed in the United States of America

10 9 8 7 6 5 4 3 2 1

To Our Readers: We have done our best to make sure all Internet Addresses in this book were active and appropriate when we went to press. However, the author and the publisher have no control over and assume no liability for the material available on those Internet sites or on other Web sites they may link to. Any comments or suggestions can be sent by e-mail to comments@enslow.com or to the address on the back cover.

♻ Enslow Publishers, Inc., is committed to printing our books on recycled paper. The paper in every book contains 10% to 30% post-consumer waste (PCW). The cover board on the outside of each book contains 100% PCW. Our goal is to do our part to help young people and the environment too!

Illustration Credits: Adrián Palacios and Patricio Velez, University of Valparaíso, Chile, pp. 31, 34; Dr. James F. Hare, Associate Professor, Department of Zoology, University of Manitoba, pp. 6, 7, 9, 11; Dr. Kenneth Catania, Associate Professor, Department of Biological Sciences, Vanderbilt University, pp. 16, 18; Jupiterimages Corporation, p. 28; Martina Nagy, Institute for Zoology, University of Erlangen, Germany, p. 21; Mirjam Knörnschild, Institute for Zoology, University of Erlangen, Germany, p. 22; National Eye Institute, National Institute of Health, p. 36; Washington University School of Medicine in St. Louis, p. 26.

Cover Illustration: Washington University School of Medicine in St. Louis.

★ CONTENTS ★

1
Whispering Squirrels
Page 5

2
Underwater "Sniffing" Is Bubble-icious
Page 13

3
Baby Bats Babble
Page 19

4
Sounds Very "Mice"
Page 25

5
The Degu's Double-Take Secret
Page 30

★

Chapter Notes . . . Page 40

Glossary . . . Page 45

Further Reading and
Internet Addresses . . . Page 47

Index . . . Page 48

★

ENTER THE WORLD OF ANIMAL SECRETS!

This volume of *Animal Secrets Revealed!* will solve many intriguing mysteries of some of the smallest rodents, insectivores, and bats.

Richardson's ground squirrels, also called gophers, communicate with each other very loudly, but sometimes they whisper. Canadian scientists wondered what they were saying. The bizarre-looking star-nosed mole stands out for its unique nose that keeps surprising scientists. Scientists from Germany have discovered that tiny but very loud sac-winged bats also share an important trait with people, especially with human babies. Can you guess what it is? In the United States, scientists studying lab mice have discovered that these little rodents have something unexpected in common with people, particularly when males are looking for a date. And in the country of Chile, scientists have uncovered that a distant relative of the hamster, the little furry degu, has eyes that perceive what people would never see. Enter the world of animal secrets!

1
WHISPERING SQUIRRELS

James Hare was standing in a grassy open field with a tan hat in his hand. He was facing a group of Richardson's ground squirrels. He tossed the hat like a Frisbee toward "6-spots," one of the female squirrels. The squirrel watched the hat land on the ground in front of her. Then, 6-spots stood up facing the hat, flicked her tail a few times, and produced a series of sounds like chirps and whistles, some ending with "chucks."[1] When the other squirrels heard these alarm calls, they became vigilant or alert. They stood up on their two hind legs, sometimes slouching, sometimes straight. Some even ran back to their burrow! All these events happened in just a few seconds.[2]

The Mystery Call

James Hare has been throwing his hat at Richardson's ground squirrels for years. He is not playing with the squirrels; he wants to understand how these small

David Wilson and colleague Jennifer Sloan release a Richardson's ground squirrel in its natural environment. Notice the holes in the ground, which are entrances to the squirrels' burrows.

rodents warn each other about approaching predators. Hare has observed that the squirrels react to the hat the same way they react to real predators, such as badgers, weasels, eagles, hawks, and falcons.

Ground squirrels are in more danger when young, but adults are also at risk. It seems that to help protect each other from the rapacious hunters, Richardson's ground squirrels have come up with loud alarm calls to warn each other of approaching dangers.[3]

But one day, Hare observed that 6-spots produced a whisper of a call. Even though 6-spots stood up straight, flicked her tail, and opened her mouth, Hare could only hear a faint sound of rushing air coming from the little rodent's mouth. Did the squirrel lose her voice or was this a new call Hare could not hear?[4]

> **Science Tongue Twister:**
> *Richardson's ground squirrels are known by scientists as* **Spermophilus richardsonii.**

The Bat Connection

Hare kept watching the squirrels. He noticed that, besides 6-spots, many other squirrels whispered calls when he tossed his tan hat at them. He also noticed that the squirrels switched back and forth between audible calls and whisper calls. He realized then that the squirrels had not lost their voices; they just chose between loud and silent calls. Maybe Hare could not hear the whisper call because it was outside the human hearing range.[5]

Hare wondered if ultrasound was involved. Ultrasound is a high-pitched sound that people cannot hear, but many other animals can use it for various purposes. For example, bats are well-known for using ultrasound to locate their prey. They also use it to avoid obstacles while flying in the dark.

Hare was lucky that summer. One of his visiting students from Germany loved to study bats and had her own "bat detector." A bat detector is a device that allows people to "hear" bat ultrasounds. It works by lowering the pitch so human ears can hear the sounds. Hare borrowed the bat detector from his student. The next time he saw a squirrel "whispering" a call he could not hear, he pointed the bat detector at it.[6]

Close-up of a Richardson's ground squirrel in a slouch-vigilant posture. This is a medium-alert posture adopted during ultrasonic calls.

Ultra-Squirrels

Eureka! The squirrel was producing ultrasonic calls.[7] After studying the calls further, Hare and his colleague David Wilson discovered that the ultrasonic calls lasted a very short time, just 225 milliseconds (2/10 of a second). Although both audible and ultrasonic calls last about the same time, ultrasonic calls have a higher pitch. When compared to an audible sound, the calls were as loud to the squirrel as a bus passing you while you are on the sidewalk.[8] But, what was their purpose?

Other animals closely related to squirrels use ultrasonic calls to communicate. Mice, for example, are rodents like the squirrels and use ultrasonic calls. Mouse pups cry out ultrasonic whimpers when they are cold. Their mothers hear their cries and respond by looking for them and bringing them to a warm place.[9]

> **Meet the Scientists:**
>
> *James Hare and David Wilson are zoologists from the University of Manitoba, Canada. They are very interested in animal behavior and acoustic communication.*

Hare and Wilson wondered what was the purpose of Richardson's ground squirrels' ultrasonic calls. The squirrels produced the call after the scientists tossed a hat at them. Could the squirrels be alerting others of approaching danger, just like the audible calls do? How could Wilson and Hare prove that the whispers were alarm calls?

Record and Play Back

Wilson and Hare used special equipment to record and play back ultrasonic calls. Wilson brought the equipment to the grassy fields inhabited by the squirrels and recorded numerous ultrasonic calls. He then went back to his lab and used computer programs to select the best recordings. These were the recordings that sounded very clear and had little noise from the environment.

Wilson drove sixty kilometers (thirty-seven miles) away from the recording site and played the ultrasound recordings back to a different group of Richardson's ground squirrels. After testing the ultrasound playbacks on nineteen squirrels, Wilson and Hare were convinced. The ultrasounds were alarm calls.

After hearing the playbacks, the squirrels adopted vigilant or alert postures, like they did when they heard audible alarm calls. However, when the squirrels heard the ultrasonic alarms, they showed only a low-alert posture (down on all fours with the head up). The squirrels were alert but like they were hiding from a predator. In comparison, when squirrels heard audible calls, they usually

Close-up of a Richardson's ground squirrel in a low-vigilance or low-alert posture usually adopted after an ultrasonic call. Notice that although its four paws are on the ground, the squirrel is looking up checking its surroundings.

showed either a slouch alert posture or high-vigilance alert posture (standing very straight on their hind legs).[10] They were ready to run from a very close predator!

Two Good Things About Ultrasound

Richardson's ground squirrels are the first animals known to use ultrasound to alert others of their kind of an upcoming danger. Wilson and Hare had another question. Why would the furry rodents use an ultrasonic alarm call instead of an audible call?

The problem with raising an audible alarm call to warn family and neighbors is that predators can hear it too. Then, predators can easily locate, and eat, the caller. But this is not the case for ultrasonic calls. Ultrasound has two characteristics that sometimes make it a better alarm call than audible sounds.

First, unlike audible calls all predators can hear, ultrasonic calls

SQUIRREL ULTRASOUND FACTS

1. Babysitting, Ultra-Style

Adult squirrels watching over nearby juvenile squirrels produce ultrasonic alarm calls to warn them of an approaching predator, without alerting the predator. The juveniles are able to recognize the alarm calls soon after birth and respond by swiftly running back to their burrow![11]

2. High Pitch

The pitch or wave frequency of sounds is indicated in hertz. One hertz represents one sound wave per second. People hear sounds up to about fifteen thousand hertz or fifteen kilohertz. Falcons, hawks, and owls cannot hear sounds with a pitch higher than about twelve kilohertz. The ultrasonic alarm calls produced by Richardson's ground squirrels are about forty-eight kilohertz.[12]

A Richardson's ground squirrel displaying a high-vigilance (or high-alert) posture, rising above the grass to closely inspect its environment after an audible call.

are outside the hearing range of some of the squirrels' predators. Hawks, falcons, and owls cannot hear ultrasonic sounds. However, other predators like coyotes, dogs, cats, and foxes are not deaf to ultrasound as long as they are close enough to hear it.[13] Here is where the second characteristic of ultrasound becomes important.

Ultrasound does not reach as far as audible sound. It travels about eight meters (twenty-six feet) away from the animal making the ultrasound. Audible calls, on the other hand, travel farther. Most humans can hear them about one hundred meters (three hundred thirty feet) away from the caller.[14]

If a badger is more than eight meters (twenty-six feet) away from a squirrel, then it will not be able to hear the ultrasonic alarm call. When predators are far away, squirrels most likely produce ultrasonic calls so only nearby squirrels, and not predators, can hear the warning.

But if the ultra-sensitive predator is closer than eight meters (twenty-six feet), then it will hear the ultrasonic alarm loud and clear. A predator that close represents a greater threat. In this case the rodents use loud audible calls, alerting all squirrels near and far of the high threat of a nearby predator.

Hare and Wilson discovered the secret of the whispering squirrels. The whispers are ultrasonic alarm calls that the rodents use to alert nearby squirrels without risking being heard by an approaching predator.

Do You Know the Noise?

Richardson's ground squirrels are very good at listening and identifying sounds from their environment. If they were not, they might not survive too long. The squirrels have a wonderful ability to recognize specific individuals by voice. They can also recognize the level of urgency in different calls.

How is your ability to identify sounds?

Materials
★ blindfold
★ coins
★ four pencils or pens
★ notebook paper
★ big book
★ ice and glass
★ plates and silverware
★ a friend or two

Procedure
1. Ask a friend who does not mind being blindfolded to do this experiment (some people do not like the feeling).
2. Making sure your friend cannot see, ask what made the following noises: drop the coins on the floor; drop the pencils (pens) on the table; drop the big book on the floor; crumble the notebook paper; add four ice cubes to the glass; place silverware on top of a plate.
3. How many sounds did your friend guess correctly? Come up with different sounds and ask your friend to test you next!

2
UNDERWATER "SNIFFING" IS BUBBLE-ICIOUS

Kenneth Catania is standing in his lab looking into an aquarium. There, chewing on an earthworm and surrounded by a mixture of potting soil and peat moss is one of the most bizarre creatures in the animal kingdom, the star-nosed mole.

The name tells it all. The star-shaped nose makes this mole stand out among not only other moles, but all other animals too. No other animal has a nose like this; there have to be a few secrets hidden in this unique scent-sniffing organ!

Wonder Nose

Twenty-two fleshy appendages or finger-like extensions circle the strange nose forming the "star." The points of the star are never still. They are a constant blur of motion as the hamster-size mole explores its environment, usually looking for food. The appendages surround two orifices or holes, which are

Meet the Scientists:

Kenneth Catania is a neuroscientist (an expert on the nervous system), at Vanderbilt University, Nashville, Tennessee. He is interested in very special and unusual animal sensory organs.

the actual nose. But the appendages are not part of the scent-detecting or olfactory system of the mole. Neither are they an extra hand to gather food. The star is a "touch organ" more sensitive than any other known.[1]

Besides having an odd-looking nose, the star-nosed mole is different from other moles in that it spends much of its time in water. It is the only mole that prefers to live in wet marshes and bogs, rather than on well-drained, dry land. Some of its tunnels open into fresh water streams.[2]

In water, as well as on land, the mole is constantly exploring, looking for insect larvae and worms to eat. It wriggles its star-shaped nose at incredible speed and traps fast-food snacks constantly. And this is what fascinated Catania. How does the star-nosed mole find its food underwater?

The Mystery Bubbles

For years, Catania has closely observed how star-nosed moles feed underwater as they swim in the aquariums he keeps in the lab. This has not been an easy task. The moles are masters at eating fast—very fast. They eat so fast that the human eye cannot see it clearly. So Catania decided to slow down the action.

First, Catania stuck food, like pieces of night crawlers (earthworms), to the bottom of the tank. Then he added about six centimeters (2.4 inches) of water to the tank and placed moles inside. Using a high-speed video camera pointed at the bottom of the clear glass aquarium, he watched the mole searching for food underwater. Then, Catania slowed down the film and saw something he had not seen before.[3]

As the moles were touching the pieces of earthworms, wriggling their star-shaped nose around the food, they were also blowing bubbles out of their noses. Then they sucked the bubbles right back in. Some of the bubbles touched the earthworms before going back into their noses. The moles pushed air out and sucked it back in about ten times per second. Try to do it yourself, just like a rat or mouse would sniff a scent.[4]

Catania was intrigued. Were the moles actually "sniffing" under-water? All experts believed that air-breathing mammals could not use their sense of smell underwater. If you sniff while your head is underwater, you will just get a squirt of water up your nose that will make you cough. It does not seem possible to smell things while underwater. Or does it? Have these weird-looking moles found a way to make it possible?

Follow That Scent!

One of the things mammals living on land use their sense of smell for is to track down prey. They sniff the ground or the air looking

WHERE THE STAR-NOSED MOLE LIVES

This one-of-a-kind mole lives mostly alone throughout much of the northeastern United States and eastern Canada. Scientists have found it as far northeast as Labrador and Nova Scotia. It has been seen southwest through Wisconsin, Indiana, and Ohio. Along the Atlantic coast, the mole enjoys wetlands as far south as Georgia.[5]

Close-up of the odd-looking star-nosed mole. Its nose is circled by 22 finger-like appendages with an exquisite sense of touch. Notice the mole's large paws with very long claws made for digging in muddy soil.

for a scent left by their prey and follow it, hoping it will lead them to lunch. Catania decided to find out if sniffing with the mystery bubbles would also help the moles track their prey.

First, Catania dragged an earthworm along a thin channel on a see-through plastic platform placed on the bottom of the aquarium. This would leave the worm's scent all over the channel. The platform was covered with six centimeters of water as before.

Then, he covered the earthworm's scent with a grid that prevented the wriggly nose appendages from touching the scent. Only bubbles could go in and out of the grid and touch the scent. Using this setup, the moles would only be able to use the mystery bubbles to find the prey, but not their supersensitive "star." At the end of the scent trail was a reward (the earthworm), in a hole not covered by the grid.[6]

Catania let the mole dive into the aquarium through a tunnel coming from the surface. He videotaped its behavior using the high-speed camera. Then, he slowed down the tape and watched the video. When the mole dived into the water, it began blowing bubbles and wriggling its "star" at an incredibly high speed, swaying its head right and left. Then, the mole found the scent trail in the channel. It followed the scent underwater, blowing and sucking bubbles through the grid. Finally, it grabbed the worm at the end of the trail.[7] The mole swiftly swam back to the surface through the tunnel and ate the worm.

Five moles succeeded in following the scent and finding their reward in seventeen out of twenty tries. Some moles succeeded in finding the reward in all their attempts. That is an 85 to 100 percent accuracy rate at finding their lunch using the mystery bubbles![8] When Catania used a grid that was too small for the bubbles to go through, the moles found the reward in only about half of the attempts.

THE HUNGRIEST MOLE IS THE FASTEST EATER

The star-nosed mole is always hungry. Day and night, this little furry mole is looking for its favorite food in mud or water. The fleshy nose appendages are the most sensitive touch organs ever found in an animal. Moles wriggle their stars nonstop, feeling for worms, insects, and insect larvae. The creatures blow bubbles and swing their heads right and left. When the amazing nose finds a snack, the mole gobbles it up at lightning speed. Catania has timed the mole's actions. He found that after touching a small piece of food, the mole took only about 2/10 of a second to identify it and eat it! That is faster than the time it takes a car driver to hit the brakes after seeing a traffic light turn red (this reaction takes about 7/10 of a second).[9]

Scent in a Bubble

Catania thinks that when the air bubbles come in contact with an object underwater, an odorant, or "smell" molecule, from the object mixes with the air inside the bubble. Then, when the mole sucks the bubbles back into its nose, the odorant makes contact with the olfactory sensors.[10] In a fraction of a second the mole knows that it is on the right track to something bubble-icious!

Close-up of a star-nosed mole sniffing underwater. See the two air bubbles coming out of its nose as the tiny mole explores the bottom of the aquarium.

3
BABY BATS BABBLE

irjam Knörnschild is sitting quietly on a hanging bridge in La Selva ("The Forest"), a research station in the rain forest of Costa Rica. She has a series of high-tech gadgets by her side. She has a highly sensitive digital microphone attached to a parabolic reflector (a device that looks like a dish). She has a laptop computer with advanced programs to record and analyze sound, as well as a paper notebook in which to write notes. Mirjam Knörnschild is listening to and recording the calls of one very small insect-eating mammal, the sac-winged bat.

Tiny and Loud

This dark-gray bat is very small. Its total body length (counting the tail) is eight centimeters (about 3.2 inches) for the biggest sac-winged bats. This is about as long as a small cell phone. But in comparison to a

Meet the Scientists:

Mirjam Knörnschild is a zoologist who loves bats and is very interested in animal behavior and acoustic (sound) communication. She works at the University of Erlangen-Nuremberg, Germany.

cell phone, these bats are much lighter. They weigh about nine grams (3/10 ounce).[1] This is as much as four dimes together! (Believe it or not, it is not a record-breaker; there are still much smaller bats out there!)

Sac-winged bats may be only as long as a cell phone and as light as four dimes, but they are one of the most talkative bats. The adults not only use calls for echolocation to find insects to eat, they also communicate with each other. They use barks, screeches, chatters, whistles, and trills. Adult bats use specific types of calls for particular situations. Males produce trills, for example, when they are looking for a mate.[2]

But it is not the adult bats Mirjam (who prefers to be called by her first name) and her colleagues are interested in. They are interested in the bat pups. It turns out that the pups are very noisy too. But what are they saying?

How to Eavesdrop on a Baby Bat

Mirjam had two reasons to travel all the way from her home in Germany to Costa Rica to study sac-winged bats. The bats in La

WHERE THE NAME COMES FROM

Sac-winged bats got their name from a sac or pouch they have on their wings. The sac contains individual scents, something like a particular perfume that identifies each bat. Male bats open the pouch and fan the odor or smell toward females when looking for a mate. They also use their perfume to mark their territory.[3]

Mirjam Knörnschild during a recording session of baby bats. These babies made this cabin their home (below). At left, a sac-winged baby bat is roosting.

WHERE THE SAC-WINGED BATS LIVE

This tiny but very vocal bat lives in tropical forests from Mexico through Central America, on some Caribbean islands (Trinidad and Tobago), and in Brazil.[4]

Selva live in a natural environment and they are used to people. Even the pups are familiar with having scientists around them.

These allowed Mirjam to place her high-tech microphones and other equipment very close to the bats. She placed the gadgets within seven meters (about twenty-three feet) of the baby bats without disturbing them.[5]

Sac-winged bats live together in large groups, called harems, that include one adult male, females, and pups. They like to roost or perch on tree limbs and on the

Up close and personal with a baby sac-winged bat perched on metal mesh.

walls of buildings. Most of these places are very dark.[6]

To eavesdrop directly on a particular baby bat roosting in a dark place, Mirjam mounted an infrared pointer on the microphone. People cannot see infrared light with their naked eyes. Mirjam used a night-vision device to make sure that the microphone was pointing directly at that particular pup. This allowed Mirjam to record baby bat sounds without disturbing the environment with flashlights.[7]

Patiently and quietly Mirjam recorded the calls produced by eleven baby bats. Then she analyzed the pups' calls using the programs on her computer. Mirjam was surprised at what she found.

Goo-Goo, Ga-Ga, Bat-Style

Sac-winged bat pups are very loud and produce many types of calls. They often utter special "isolation calls" when separated from their mothers. But Mirjam discovered that the pups also utter all the vocalizations or calls produced by the adults. However, unlike the

NOW YOU HEAR IT, NOW YOU DON'T

Sac-winged bats utter calls that are both audible and silent to people. Mirjam explains: "Barks, chatters, and trills are normally not audible to human ears because they are in the ultrasonic range (their pitch is too high for people to hear it). Screeches and whistles can be heard if you have keen ears. Isolation calls and territorial calls are clearly audible."[8]

adults that use specific sounds for specific situations (like trills only during courtship or looking for a mate), baby bats combined the different sounds any which way they wanted.[9]

Mirjam was intrigued. The calls produced by the pups reminded her of human baby babbling, the sounds babies make when they are learning to talk. "It occurred to me while looking at the sonograms or graphic representations of the sounds recorded from bat pups. They combine adult sounds into long strings of calls, just like human babies combine different syllables into babbling bouts," said Mirjam.[10] The nonsense string of sounds produced by the baby bats seems like the bat version of human baby babbling.

Mirjam thinks that babbling might help the pups train the muscles used to speak like adults. Babbling might also provide practice combining syllables into specific sounds. Before Mirjam's discovery, only human babies, pygmy marmoset pups, and many baby songbirds were known to babble.[11] She believes she has uncovered the baby bat secret. It is possible that the more they screech, trill, whistle, chatter, and bark, the better they will "speak" when they are grown.

4
SOUNDS VERY "MICE"

Tim Holy is setting a microphone inside a mouse cage in his lab. He is getting ready to record little-known sounds uttered by this common rodent. Holy is not interested in recording the easy-to-hear squeaking sounds of mice; he wants to record sounds humans cannot hear.

Scientists already had discovered that mice produce ultrasonic or high-pitch sounds, as do bats, whales, some insects, and other rodents such as Richardson's ground squirrels. But nobody had analyzed the sounds up close.[1]

Holy knew that when a male mouse meets a female mouse, he produces ultrasonic sounds. These sounds have a very high pitch, between thirty and one hundred ten kilohertz.[2] People can hear sounds up to fifteen kilohertz. We cannot perceive ultrasound because it is outside our hearing range. Thanks to modern technology, however, scientists have now overcome this limitation. They have learned to record and change ultrasonic sounds so they can hear and study them.

Smell and Sound

To study the high-pitch sounds male mice produce when they are close to female mice, Holy did not place a male and a female together in the same cage. He placed a cotton swab soaked with female mouse urine inside a cage with a male mouse. The urine contains chemicals called pheromones that tell the male mouse that a female is close by.[3]

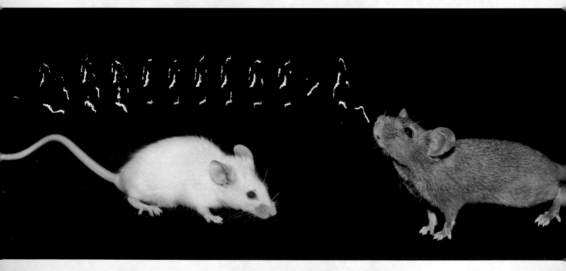

A male mouse "singing" to a female mouse. The lines drawn as coming from the mouse's mouth provide a visual representation of the ultrasonic notes sung by the male. Note that there are groups of "notes" (or lines) in a specific pattern. The patterns repeat with silent pauses or spaces in between. The higher the mark, the higher the pitch.

When Holy placed the urine-soaked swab in the cage, the male mouse scurried over and touched the swab with its nose. Female pheromones entered a special organ inside of the mouse's nose: the vomeronasal organ. It looks like a thin, short tube. Inside this organ, numerous nerves send signals to the brain when they detect pheromones.[4] Every time the male mouse sensed the female pheromones with his vomeronasal organ, he produced high-pitched sounds.

Holy was interested in understanding how pheromones prompt mice to make ultrasounds. He knew that whatever the pheromones did, they acted on the brain. He hoped to understand what happens inside the brain when pheromones make the mouse utter ultrasounds. In the end, however, he ended up discovering something completely different.[5]

An Unexpected Discovery

Holy and his colleague Zhongsheng Guo set up to work on the ultrasounds first. They wanted to be able to hear them just like a mouse would. Guo is very skilled at developing computer programs. He created programs that changed the sounds so scientists could hear them and study them note by note.

Their first approach was to alter the ultrasounds by slowing them down. Holy and Guo could hear the mouse ultrasonic calls, but they were too slow to reveal their real rhythm. They sounded like low, random whistles.[6]

The mouse is a very common rodent, not only in science labs, but in many other natural and human-made environments.

Guo wrote another computer program to reduce the chirps' pitch to the scientists' hearing level, but without changing the rhythm. Surprise! "It sounded much like a bird song," said Holy.[7]

The scientists discovered that these mouse ultrasounds were not made of a single note repeated over and over. Surprisingly, the songs were more complex than that. Holy and Guo decided to study them more.

They analyzed the ultrasonic songs of forty-five mice and found that their songs were made of notes of different pitches.

BORN SINGING OR SCHOOLED?

Holy and Guo wonder if mice are like birds when it comes to their singing abilities. Birds learn their songs by listening to adult males nearby. Do mice learn to sing by listening to other mice? Or are they born already knowing their songs? It is still an open question.[8]

Holy and Guo studied the ultrasonic singing abilities of forty-five male mice. They discovered that each mouse sings slightly different songs, adding a personal touch to their love songs.[9]

The pitch changed following a pattern and there were pauses spacing the groups of pitches over time. These are definite musical properties, just like those found in bird songs.[10]

You can listen to a mouse and a bird song for comparison by visiting the Web Addresses on page 47.

Mice Are Nice

Even though Holy and Guo had not planned on it, they uncovered the secret of the silent mouse calls. When the little male rodents feel the presence of a potential mate nearby, they sing like a bird. The songs are ultrasonic—just for the female mouse's ears. But thanks to advanced computer programs developed by Holy and Guo, now you can hear the mouse calls too.

The scientists think that the male mice's melodies are love songs or serenades. Their purpose seems to be to attract females. This is the first time that male mice had been known to sing for their mates! Welcome mice to the singing club of birds, whales, bats, and people!

5
THE DEGU'S DOUBLE-TAKE SECRET

drián Palacios is preparing a little rodent called a degu (DE-goo) for a special "eye exam." He has given the furry rodent some anesthesia, a drug to make it sleep for a while. While the little degu sleeps, Palacios uses special eyedrops to dilate, or make wider, the degu's pupils. Then he can study the light-sensitive retina.[1] The retina is the area at the back of the eye that can sense light and pass on visual information to the brain.

The eye exam is not like the one people receive at the eye doctor's (ophthalmologist) office to determine how well they see. Palacios does not want to know if the little degu needs glasses. He is curious to find out what colors degus can see.

Beyond Violet

Color vision is common among animals. People, primates, birds, fish, and reptiles see many colors.

Two degus on top of the researchers' paperwork.

Colors make up white light. You see proof of this when white light passes through a prism and the colors separate, forming a rainbow. Light and the colors that form it are a type of radiation or wave-like energy called "electromagnetic" radiation. The colors that we see with our eyes, called the "visible spectrum," are only a small part of a larger spectrum or family of electromagnetic radiation. The family ranges from gamma rays (produced by some radioactive materials) to the radio waves you hear in your car. Like all electromagnetic radiation, light travels like the waves that form in a pond when you drop a stone in it. Each color has a specific wavelength that makes it different from the others. However, they all have something in common. All the colors and electromagnetic radiation travel at the same speed, three hundred thousand kilometers per second (or one hundred eighty-six thousand miles per second), which is commonly known as the speed of light.[2]

However, dichromatic color vision or seeing only two colors ("di" means two and "chromatic" means color) is the most common form of color vision among mammals. Most mammals see blue and green.[3] But this is not all animals can see.

There are "colors" people cannot see, but other animals can. People see colors that range from violet to red. Each color has a particular wavelength. Violet and blue have the shortest wavelengths at about four hundred nanometers, while the wavelength of red is about six hundred fifty nanometers. But there is another "color" beyond violet. It is called "ultraviolet" or UV light.[4]

UV light comes from the sun. People cannot "see" UV light with their eyes like they see colors, and they cannot feel it either. However, UV light can damage skin. (Sun burn is caused by infrared light radiation, not UV light.)[5] Experts always recommend

Science Tongue Twister:
Scientists call degus Octodon degus.

HOW SMALL IS A NANOMETER?

To imagine how small a nanometer is, pretend that you have a string one meter long (about 3.3 feet). Now, divide the string into one million equal parts. Each one of these sections is one millionth of a meter (a micrometer; "micro" means a millionth). Finally, divide one millionth of a meter into one thousand equal parts. Each one of them is a nanometer. One nanometer is too small for our naked eyes to see. Gamma rays have the shortest wavelength, about one-tenth of a nanometer or less, while radio waves may be many meters long.[6]

protecting our skin from UV light with clothing and sunscreen lotions and not staying too long in the sun.

Animals and UV Light

People may not be able to see UV light, but many animals can. Numerous insects and birds can see it. Marsupials, bats, and many rodents, including mice, rats, and gerbils can see UV light.[7] The main question scientists have is, how do rodents use UV vision?

Palacios is from the South American country of Chile. He wanted to know what colors little degus see. This plant-eating rodent lives in groups all over Chile, from the coast to the mountains. Can degus see UV light like other rodents? And if they can, why is seeing beyond violet important for survival?

What Degus See

Palacios teamed up with Leo Peichl, a German scientist with much experience in how animals see. Together with other scientists in the Chilean lab, Peichl and Palacios gave the degu a special eye exam.

33

A close-up of a degu. It is standing on a color chart right on top of the "colors" it sees best.

FROM LIGHT TO IMAGE

Light waves may be very small, but they are capable of making "an impression" on the retina—literally. Light waves coming from an object enter the eye and are absorbed by special cells in the retina called "photoreceptor cells." These cells contain "visual pigments," molecules that are activated when hit by light. This activation is used to form an image of the object on the retina, like what you see on the film of an old-fashioned camera. The activated cells also transmit signals to the brain, which puts all the information together in a way that makes sense to us.[8]

While the degu slept and its pupils were dilated, the scientists recorded an "electroretinogram." This eye exam tests the effect of different lights, from UV to red, on the retina. The test determines which lights are able to trigger a response in the retina. The lights that trigger a response are the ones the animal can sense.[9]

While the degu slept, lights flashed on its retina and electronic equipment recorded the retina's response. When the scientists analyzed the results, they discovered that degus have dichromatic vision (they see only two colors). One is green and the other is UV. Just like other rodents, little degus see UV light.[10] Palacios and Peichl wondered: How is UV vision useful to degus' survival in Chile?

Follow the UV-Bright Sign!

Scientists know that an animal's or plant's abilities are important for survival in their particular environment. For example, having the ability to see red and yellow colors allows some primates like gorillas and chimpanzees to find the colorful fruits they love to eat. Palacios and Peichl wanted to know why having UV vision was useful to degus.

To answer the question they tested many things in the degus' environment that might have UV color or reflect UV light.

Since degus are herbivores, the scientists checked if the plants the animals eat reflect UV light. If they did, having UV vision would help degus find food.

The scientists also thought about how degus behave. Degus live in groups and move around a lot, following the same trails.

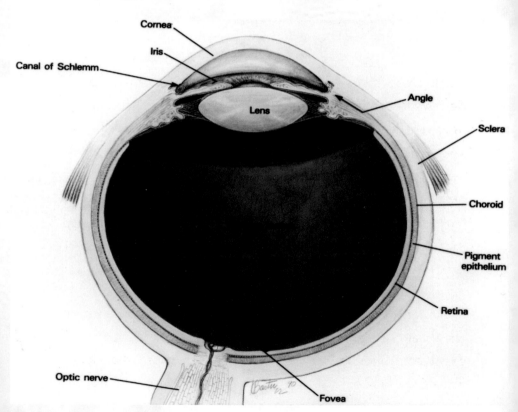

How a human eye looks on the inside. All animals' eyes have the same general structure.

Along the trails, degus leave mini-urine puddles marking the trail. The scientists even tested the soil and rocks on degus' paths.

Since the scientists cannot see UV light, they used an instrument called a "spectrometer." It measures the light objects reflect, from UV to red. The spectrometer revealed a very interesting clue about why degus have UV vision.

Plants, soil, and rocks do not reflect UV light (they reflect other colors). But degus' urine is UV-bright! It is the brightest when fresh and it becomes less and less UV-bright as it dries. Once dried, it looks just like the soil and rocks it is on.[11]

Double-Flagged Marks

Palacios, Peichl, and their colleagues have solved the little degu's secret. Degus' ability to "see" UV light allows the little rodents to perceive fresh urine as bright marks on a trail. Fresh, UV-bright urine tells degus that the trail has been used recently by others. To join their group, little degus just have to follow the bright urine mini-puddles on the ground. Urine also has strong scents that degus can smell. By using both visual and "smelly" clues in their fresh urine, degus make sure they keep their families together and increase their chances of survival.[12]

Colors All Around You

The colors of your clothes, shoes, hair, and everything else around you usually result from the way light is absorbed and reflected by the object. Your shirt looks red, for example, because when light illuminates the shirt, it absorbs all the colors in white light except red, which is reflected or bounced back to our eyes.

When you color a picture with crayons, markers, or paint, you usually start with many different colors. If you just have three colors, like red, yellow, and blue, for example, you may think that you are not very lucky. With just three colors you will not be able to make your picture very colorful, right? Wrong! The science of light and color is here to the rescue.

You just need three colors, called primary colors, which you can mix in numerous ways to create different colors. In this experiment you will stretch your imagination to create various colorful designs with just three colors.

Materials

★ three to six white paper plates
★ red, yellow, and blue crayons, markers, or paint
★ sharpened pencil
★ ruler

Procedure

1. Using the pencil and the ruler, divide the plate into eight equal parts, like a pizza divided into slices.

2. Color each "slice of the pizza" with a different color—red, yellow, or blue.

3. Use the sharpened pencil to poke a hole in the center of the plate. Push the pencil through the hole and center the plate on the pencil.

4. Spin the plate around the pencil with your hand.

5. Spin it faster and faster.

Did you see new colors? Are the colors "mixing" in front of your eyes? What would happen if you drew a different design on the plate instead of a pizza shape?

What do you get if you mix two different primary colors on a separate piece of white paper?

Mix red and yellow.

Mix yellow and blue.

Mix blue and red.

These are called secondary colors.

★ CHAPTER NOTES ★

Chapter 1. Whispering Squirrels

1. Jennifer L. Sloan, David R. Wilson, and James F. Hare, "Functional Morphology of Richardson's Ground Squirrel, Spermophilus richardsonii, Alarm Calls: The Meaning of Chirps, Whistles, and Chucks," *Animal Behaviour*, Vol. 70, October 2005, pp. 937–944.

2. Personal interview with Dr. James Hare, April 12, 2007.

3. David R. Wilson and James F. Hare, "The Adaptive Utility of Richardson's Ground Squirrel (Spermophilus richardsonii) Short-range Ultrasonic Alarm Signals," *Canadian Journal of Zoology*, Vol. 84, No. 9, September 1, 2006, p. 1322.

4. Personal interview with Dr. James Hare.

5. Ibid.

6. Ibid.

7. David R. Wilson and James F. Hare, "Ground Squirrel Uses Ultrasonic Alarms," *Nature*, Vol. 430, July 29, 2004, p. 523.

8. Personal interview with Dr. James Hare.

9. Gillian Sales and David Pye, *Ultrasonic Communication by Animals* (London: Chapman & Hall, Ltd., 1974), p. 150.

10. Personal interview with Dr. David Wilson, April 10, 2007.

11. Wilson and Hare, "The Adaptive Utility of Richardson's Ground Squirrel," p. 1323.

12. Ibid.

13. Wilson and Hare, "The Adaptive Utility of Richardson's Ground Squirrel," p. 1323.

14. Personal interview with Dr. James Hare.

Chapter 2. Underwater "Sniffing" Is Bubble-icious

1. Kenneth C. Catania, "The Nose Takes a Starring Role," *Scientific American*, July 2002, pp. 54–59.

2. T. L. Yates, "The Mole That Keeps Its Nose Clean," *Natural History*, Vol. 92, No. 11, November 1983, p. 55.

3. Kenneth C. Catania, "Underwater 'Sniffing' by Semi-aquatic Mammals," *Nature*, Vol. 444, December 21, 2006, pp. 1024–1025.

4. Ibid., p. 1024.

5. Yates, p. 55.

6. Catania, "Underwater 'Sniffing' by Semi-aquatic Mammals," p. 1024.

7. Ibid.

8. Ibid., pp. 1024–1025.

9. David F. Salisbury, "Star-Nosed Mole Has Moves That Put the Best Magician to Shame," *Exploration*, Vanderbilt University, February 2, 2005, <http://www.vanderbilt.edu/exploration/stories/starnosedmole.html?search_by=star+nose+mole> (September 18, 2007).

10. David F. Salisbury, "Two Small, Semi-aquatic Mammals Blow Bubbles While Swimming and Then Inhale Them to Smell Submerged Objects," *Exploration*, Vanderbilt University, December 20, 2006, <http://exploration.vanderbilt.edu/text/

index.php?action=view_section&id=1154&story_id=
278&images=> (September 18, 2007).

Chapter 3. Baby Bats Babble

1. Wally Welker, John Irwin Johnson, and Adrianne Noe, "Greater Sac-winged (White-lined) Bat (Saccopteryx bilineata)," *Comparative Mammalian Brain Collections*, n.d., <http://www.brainmuseum.org/specimens/chiroptera/Whitelined/index.html> (November 1, 2007).

2. Mirjam Knörnschild, Oliver Behr, and Otto Von Helversen, "Babbling Behavior in the Sac-winged Bat (Saccopteryx bilineata)," *Naturwissenschaften*, Vol. 93, No. 9, September 2006, p. 453.

3. Welker, Johnson, and Noe.

4. Ibid.

5. Knörnschild, Behr, and Von Helversen, p. 452.

6. Personal interview with Dr. Mirjam Knörnschild, April 12, 2007.

7. Knörnschild, Behr, and Von Helversen, p. 453.

8. Personal interview with Dr. Mirjam Knörnschild.

9. Knörnschild, Behr, and Von Helversen, pp. 453–454.

10. Personal interview with Dr. Mirjam Knörnschild.

11. Knörnschild, Behr, and Von Helversen, p. 451.

Chapter 4. Sounds Very "Mice"

1. Michael Purdy, "Researchers Add Mice to List of Creatures That Sing in the Presence of Mates," Washington University Medical News Release, October 31, 2005,

<http://mednews.wustl.edu/news/page/normal/6040.html> (September 18, 2007).

2. Timothy E. Holy and Zhongsheng Guo, "Ultrasonic Songs of Male Mice," *PLoS Biology*, Vol. 3, No. 12, December 2005, p. 2177, <http://biology.plosjournals.org/perlserv/ ?request= get-document&doi=10.1371/journal.pbio.0030386> (October 15, 2007).

3. Ibid., p. 2178.

4. C. Wysocki, et al., "The Vomeronasal Organ: Primary Role in Mouse Chemosensory Gender Recognition," *Physiological Behavior*, Vol. 29, No. 2, August 1982, pp. 315–327.

5. Personal interview with Dr. Tim Holy, December 14, 2005.

6. Holy and Guo, p. 2178.

7. Personal interview with Dr. Tim Holy.

8. Holy and Guo, p. 2184.

9. Ibid.

10. Ibid., p. 2178.

Chapter 5. The Degu's Double-Take Secret

1. Andrés E. Chávez, Francisco Bozinovic, Leo Peichl, and Adrián Palacios, "Retinal Spectral Sensitivity, Fur Coloration, and Urine Reflectance in the Genus Octodon (Rodentia): Implications for Visual Ecology," *Investigative Ophthalmology & Visual Science*, Vol. 44, No. 5, May 2003, p. 2290.

2. Mortimer Abramowitz, Shannon H. Neaves, and Michael W. Davidson, "The Nature of Electromagnetic Radiation," *Molecular Expressions: Science, Optics and You*, August 23,

2005, <http://micro.magnet.fsu.edu/optics/lightandcolor/ elec-tromagnetic.html> (September 18, 2007).

3. Leo Peichl, "Diversity of Mammalian Photoreceptor Properties: Adaptations to Habitat and Lifestyle?" *The Anatomical Record*, Part A, 287A, Vol. 287, No. 1, November 2005, p. 1001.

4. ACEPT W3 Group, "Color and Light," Department of Physics and Astronomy, Arizona State University, December 26, 1999, <http://acept.asu.edu/PiN/rdg/color/color.shtml> (September 18, 2007).

5. Personal interview with Dr. Adrián Palacios, April 10, 2007.

6. Abramowitz, Neaves, and Davidson.

7. Personal interview with Dr. Leo Peichl, April 10, 2007.

8. Ibid.

9. Chávez, Bozinovic, Peichl, and Palacios, p. 2291.

10. Ibid., pp. 2290, 2294.

11. Ibid., pp. 2290, 2293.

12. *Max Planck Society Press Release*, "An Eye for Scent Marks," June 10, 2003, <http://www.mpg.de/english/ illustrationsDocumentation/documentation/pressReleases/ 2003/pressRelease20030610/index.html> (March 25, 2008).

★ GLOSSARY ★

anesthesia ★ A drug that reduces pain.

appendage ★ A body part that projects from the main body, such as a tail or a wing.

audible ★ Loud enough to be heard.

dichromatic ★ Having two colors.

echolocation ★ Locating an object by emitting sound and perceiving it reflected back.

grid ★ A set of crisscrossed lines.

olfactory ★ Related to the sense of smell.

pheromones ★ Chemicals produced by animals that affect the behavior of others of the same species.

predator ★ An animal that hunts, kills, and eats other animals to survive.

prey ★ An animal hunted, killed, and eaten by other animals as food.

primates ★ The group of mammals that includes humans, apes, and monkeys.

retina ★ Light-sensitive membrane in the back of the eye.

roost ★ A place where birds or bats sleep.

scent ★ An odor or smell.

sonogram ★ An image an ultrasound produces.

ultrasound ★ Sound frequencies above the normal range of human hearing.

vigilant ★ Watchful and alert.

vomeronasal organ ★ Special organ that detects pheromones.

★ FURTHER READING ★

Books

Davies, Nicola. *Extreme Animals : The Toughest Creatures on Earth.* Cambridge, Mass.: Candlewick Press, 2006.

Stonehouse, Bernard, and Esther Bertram. *How Animals Live: The Amazing World of Animals in the Wild.* New York: Scolastic, 2004.

World Book's Animals of the World, Set 4: Flying Foxes and Other Bats. Chicago: World Book, Inc., 2005.

Internet Addresses

Ana María Rodríguez's Homepage
http://www.anamariarodriguez.com/

Videos of the Star-Nosed Mole Underwater
http://www.nature.com/nature/journal/v444/n7122/suppinfo/4441024a.html)

Movie of an Alarm-Calling Richardson's Ground Squirrel
http://umanitoba.ca/science/zoology/faculty/hare/Harelab/callclip.avi

Babbling Baby Bats
http://www.livescience.com/php/video/player.php?video_id=SbilineaBabble

Compare a singing mouse to a singing bird here:
Mouse:
http://biology.plosjournals.org/archive/1545-7885/3/12/supinfo/10.1371_journal.pbio.0030386.sa004.wav

Swamp Sparrow:
http://biology.plosjournals.org/archive/1545-7885/3/12/supinfo/10.1371_journal.pbio.0030386.sa005.wav

★ INDEX ★

A
air bubble, 15–18
anesthesia, 30
aquarium, 13, 14, 16

B
bat, 7, 19, 20–25, 29, 33
bat detector, 7
bat harems, 22
bat, sac-winged, 19, 20–24

C
Catania, Kenneth, 13–18
Chile, 31–33, 35
Costa Rica, 19–20

D
Degu, 20–37
dichromatic vision, 32, 35
dilation, 30, 35

E
echolocation, 20
electromagnetic radiation, 31
electroretinogram, 35

G
gamma rays, 31, 33
Germany, 7, 20, 32
Guo, Zhongsheng, 27–29

H
Hare, James, 5–11
herbivore, 36

hertz, 10
high-vigilance (high-alert) posture, 10, 11
Holy, Tim, 25–29

I
infrared, 23, 32
isolation call, 23

K
kilohertz, 10, 25
Knörnschild, Mirjam, 19–24

L
La Selva ("The Forest"), 19, 21–22
low-alert posture, 9

M
mouse, 8, 15, 25–29, 33

N
nanometer, 32–33
night crawler, 14

O
odorant, 18
olfactory sensor, 14, 18
ophthalmologist (eye doctor), 30

P
Palacios, Adrián, 30, 32, 33, 35–37
parabolic reflector, 19
Peichl, Leo, 32, 33, 35–37

pheromone, 26, 27
photoreceptor cell, 35
pitch, 7, 8, 10, 23, 25–29

R
retina, 30, 32, 35
Richardson's ground squirrel, 5–12, 25

S
slouch-alert posture, 10
songbird, 24
spectrometer, 37
squirrel. *See* Ricardson's ground squirrel.
star-nosed mole, 13–18

U
ultrasound, 7–11, 23, 25–29
ultraviolet (UV) light, 32, 33, 35–37

V
vomeronasal organ, 27

W
wave frequency. *See* pitch.
Wilson, David, 6, 8–11
worm, 13–17